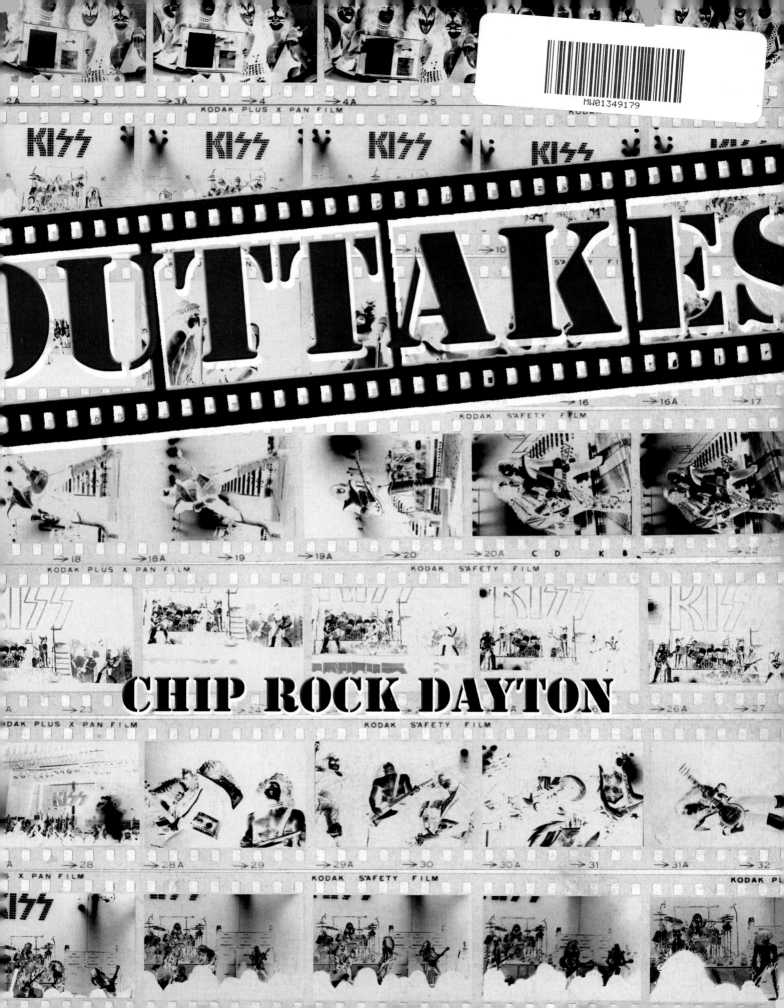

Published and distributed by
STUDIO CHIKARA
244 Fifth Avenue #2464
New York, NY 10001
www.studiochikara.net
www.stuchikara.com

First Edition

Photographs and text copyright © Chip Rock Dayton 1999 except for the following images:
the Beatles © Felix Collection/Star File, the Rolling Stones © Wilson Lindsey/Star File,
Black Sabbath & Alice Cooper © Harry Goodwin/Star File, David Bowie © Dagmar/Star File,
additional Kiss images © Bob Gruen/Star File, Steve Joester/Star File,
Glenn Brown (from the collection of James Holmes), and Martin Downes.
All other material, unless otherwise specified, is copyright © 1999 Studio Chikara.

All Rights Reserved. No part of this publication may be reproduced, stored in a retrieval system,
or transmitted in any form or by any means, electronic, mechanical, photocopying,
recording or otherwise, without the written permission of the publisher.

Robert V. Conte-Publisher
David V. Conte-Publishing Administrator
John Ostrosky-Promotions Director
Gilda Caserta, Kelly Barbieri-Transcriptions
Susan Call-Text Editor and Proofreader
Dave Streicher, Richard Lynch-Scans
Patricia Pardini-Cover Concept
Neuwirth and Associates-Book Design
Gary Esposito-Promotions Design
Wallace Collins III, Esq.-Business and Legal Affairs

Order Number: RCTP9901
ISBN (paperback) 1-890313-04-1

Order Number: RCTP9901HC
ISBN (hardcover) 1-890313-10-6

Separated, Printed and Bound in the United States of America by
Courier Companies, North Chelmsford, MA
Manufactured by Courier Kendallville, IN

For additional copies of OUTTAKES,
mail check or money order for $24.95 paperback or $59.95 hardcover + $4.00 shipping/handling to
STUDIO CHIKARA
PO BOX 527962
FLUSHING, NY 11355-5924 USA

For information to obtain prints of any image in OUTTAKES, please contact
Eric Bakken, 3817 West Delbert Ave., Spokane, WA. 99208 USA, e-mail: mr.speed@ix.netcom.com.

Studio Chikara wants your comments on OUTTAKES.
Please send them to the above address, or e-mail StuChikara@aol.com.

This book is dedicated to my two sons, John and Robby Dayton

Robby, my wife Debbie, and John at a KISS concert in 1996 at Nassau Coliseum, NY.

My special thanks to Josh McClure, Tom DeStio, Dennis Woloch, Joseph Yacoe, James Holmes, Richie Ranno, Bill Aucoin, Mary Croghan, Denis Carr, John Reed, Craig Wright, Gary Madison, Ken Zeran, Al Larson, Joe Reboh, Ronn Roxburgh, Jeff Ayers, Clint Finlayson, Eric Bakken, Serge Champagne, John Cooper, Mary Ellen McGayley, Karen Hatch Taylor, John Lesniewski, Jeff Augsburger, Gilda Caserta, Peter Dayton, and the members of KISS.

And a very special thanks to Tommy Thayer.

INTRODUCTION

IT WASN'T THE FIRST TIME I had been in the photo pit, maybe the second or third. But this time, after two or three songs, I could see the Spaceman adjusting a knob on his guitar. Then he strummed a chord to test his celestial sound. The feeling from just that one chord coming from his Marshall stacks was so awesome and powerful, it dawned on me—as I quickly glanced back at the crowd—that I was somewhere very special. As the next song started, the Starchild came toward me, leaned down and posed, just for me! He was right there—a mere fifteen inches away! It was then that I felt like a pro for the first time.

There were many such special nights and experiences, as shooting KISS became my number-one interest in life. From the pages of this book, you won't be able to hear Ace's crunching chords, Peter's machine-gun rim shots, Paul's towering vocals or Gene's through-the-body bass notes (yes, the "whummmm" of the bass goes right through you when you can touch the stage). But I hope you'll feel from the stories and photos I've collected what it's like to be lucky enough to be a KISS photographer.

Chip Rock Dayton
October 1998

Photo taken by a KISS roadie backstage at Pittsburgh Civic Center, July 1996.

EARLY YEARS

I WAS BORN in the early 1950s in Manhattan and grew up in Glen Cove, Long Island. My first memory of music was later that decade, when we became a two-car family for the first time. When it comes to the music my family listened to, I remember the cars and my father playing the radio. We had only an AM radio installed because FM wasn't around then, and tape players didn't come into existence until much later. One of the earliest songs I remember was "Purple People Eater," by Sheb Wooley, a big hit at that time.

Thanks to my dad, my interest in music blossomed. In 1961 when I was ten years old, I was excited by the Twist, introduced by Chubby Checker the year before. It was a huge fad. My dad had an open mind when it came to music. He bought the records and we played them in our basement on what was called the Victrola—an RCA Victor console that

The Beatles at Shea Stadium, New York. I'm in the upper deck behind Paul McCartney.

had a turntable, amplifier and speaker all in one box. My brother, sister and some of our friends and neighbors had fun doing the Twist. There were many other things going on in music at the time, but that was *the thing*. It was good music, too—a kind of rock 'n' roll that was more rhythm 'n' blues, but it had a good beat. I first heard of the Beatles in 1964. I saw a concert program while on the school bus—immediately I noticed their long hair. They fascinated me. Soon after, I heard either "She Loves You" or maybe "I Want To Hold Your Hand" on the radio. Those songs exploded and changed my life and my friends' lives forever. During that whole year, all anyone did was talk about the Beatles and play their music. By 1965, I was really into popular music, dances and meeting girls.

I remember the *Beatles '65* album with them on the cover holding umbrellas. Other bands looked out of place, holdovers from only a couple of years before with greaser haircuts, black pointy shoes and Fender guitars, like Elvis. Things changed quickly, but you didn't notice that when you were a kid; you lived in the present. The Beatles were exciting because of their fresh music and their unique look. One day at ice hockey practice, the coach noticed the guys' hair was starting to show under the bottom of their helmets, and he said in sort of a Brooklyn accent, "'Dem dare Beatles did a bad t'ing!"

I saw the Beatles play twice: once at a benefit at the Paramount Theater with supporting act the Shangri-Las (whose hit was "Leader of the Pack"), then again at Shea Stadium with Barry and the Remains. The Beatles wore Nehru jackets, which became an instant fashion fad. I sat in the upper deck, behind third base.

THE CONCERTS

BY THE MID-1960s, the whole British Invasion had descended upon America: Herman's Hermits, the Dave Clark Five, the Animals, Freddie and the Dreamers and countless others. I bought all their records. I was really into the Hullabaloos, who inspired a short-lived TV show called "Hullabaloo." They all had dyed blond hair and I thought they were great.

And of course, I followed the Rolling Stones. During the summer of 1965, I got the *Out of Our Heads* album, the one with "Satisfaction" on it. I saw the original Stones with Brian Jones at the Forest Hills Tennis Stadium when *Aftermath* came out. I loved "Stupid Girl." Their opening acts were the Tradewinds, whose big hit was "New York's a Lonely Town," and the McCoys, with "Hang On Sloopy."

The Stones was the first real rock concert I ever went to without my parents. They say the screaming used to drown out concerts in those days, but we had no problem hearing them at all. The Stones came into the back of the stadium in a military-type helicopter. Boy, the sound of the choppers, the sound of the crowd and the sound of the music—what an entrance!

Rolling Stones, (L to R) Charlie Watts, Brian Jones, Mick Jagger and Keith Richards, mid '60s.

From left: a young Ozzy Osbourne, Geezer Butler, Bill Ward and Tony Iommi. (If Jimi Hendrix was the best left-handed guitarist ever, I'd say Iommi is the second best.) My favorite Black Sabbath album is Master of Reality.

By 1968, I had my driver's license and a green Mustang 289 four speed. It had a Panasonic eight-track with just two speakers, but the sound was fantastic. The eight-track player was an incredible invention. For the first time, music was portable. Eight-tracks also made music programmable: you could switch through four tracks and sample each tune very fast by simply pressing a button.

Later, I started listening to the Doors, Jefferson Airplane and Big Brother and the Holding Company, but I was never a Grateful Dead fan because they just didn't appeal to me.

In the early 1970s, I gravitated toward harder rock. When the term "Heavy Metal" was supposedly coined by Lester Bangs of *Creem* magazine out of Birmingham, Michigan, it made so much sense to me—the metal strings on an electric guitar and the hard, loud music. At the time heavy metal was personified by Black Sabbath, who had come from Birmingham, England.

I became a big fan of Grand Funk Railroad when I heard an ad on the radio promoting the band's first album, *On Time*. I went right out and bought it. I loved their music—it was simple and hard, but not everyone appreciated them. Then Alice Cooper came on the scene with songs like "Eighteen." I saw Alice perform at the Academy of Music in New York City during the band's "Killer" tour. Their show had fantastic lighting and effects. It was my first experience with theatrical rock. I really loved all of it—the snake, the lighting, the effects—and the SOUND.

The author at 16-years-old

David Bowie's "Ziggy Stardust" show came to New York City's Radio City Music Hall in 1973 for two nights. Like Alice Cooper, Bowie also added incredible theatricality to rock music. This show was so long it had an intermission. Bowie played one of his ballads, "Time," on stage all by himself with only a big acoustic guitar. He looked small, but he lit up the stage. It was magical. Then after the intermission, the stage rose and the Spiders from Mars came blasting out at you. It just blew me away. I've been to hundreds of rock concerts, but that show is one of my all-time favorites.

David Bowie at Radio City Music Hall, New York.

In the early seventies, Alice Cooper was the name of the entire group. From left: my friend Glen Buxton, Dennis Dunnaway, Mike Bruce and Neal Smith with Alice in the front.

I walked out of the Cooper and Bowie shows totally satisfied, not knowing that yet another theatrical rock band would soon come along and blow them out of the water. . . .

THE BEACON

BLUE OYSTER CULT was booked to headline the New Year's Eve 1973—1974 show at the Academy of Music with three other bands. The opening band was a group called KISS. I'd never heard of them. The other two were Teenage Lust and Iggy and the Stooges. I loved Iggy and was a fan since his first album in 1969 with the song "No Fun." But none of my friends wanted to go to a rock concert on New Year's Eve, so I got on the train and went to New York City alone, wearing my rock 'n' roll jacket with some glitter and stuff on it.

I got there without a ticket. I was used to doing that; I dug the street scene with scalpers, but mostly with friends of friends who had extra tickets. Sometimes I'd pay over the ticket price, but usually I'd get in for less than the original price—or for free.

By the time I got inside, Teenage Lust was on. I had missed KISS completely, but I really didn't know who KISS was anyway, so I didn't think much of it. Still, I asked the person next to me how KISS had been on stage. He said the band had flames and explosions and that they played a great show! I began to think I had really missed something. I realized later how much I had missed that night. It was KISS' first professional gig and I missed it by about a hundred feet, standing outside the entire time looking for friends and trying to get a good ticket!

A couple of months later, I moved to San Diego—the land of sun and surf—to do a lot of surfing and to "find myself." At an Encinitas record store, I was looking through the new releases and came across KISS' first record. They had makeup on, but I didn't think it was weird like most people did. I thought it was cool right away. I started reading the credits and they mentioned some New York City recording studio. I realized they were from New York, like me. I bought the album—after all, I had nothing to lose.

I quickly went home, put the vinyl on my turntable and turned it up loud. "Strutter" came blaring through the speakers. I liked the record immediately, especially "Love Theme from KISS" and "Deuce." KISS' music was energized—even inspirational. Although there were some fast solos and some speed to the album, I felt the whole compilation kept its own pace.

I stayed in San Diego for most of 1974, supporting myself as a waiter and working at a

Kiss at the Academy of Music as photographed by Bob Gruen.

Picture by Joe Stevens

By early 1975, I was living back in New York. I saw an ad for a KISS concert at the Beacon Theater in New York. At the time the Beacon was *the* uptown venue (it still is to me). Back then there really were only two theaters: the Academy of Music on 14th Street, and the Beacon on 72nd Street and Broadway. As was the Academy, the Beacon was an old-fashioned, converted movie house with a balcony. All the seats slanted upward. I love the sound in those places—there's nothing like it, completely different than an arena. (Although KISS' reunion shows had some of the best sound I've heard in an arena, those halls had—and still have—unique acoustics.) Old theaters went out of style with the explosion of high-tech multiplexes. You can tell a converted movie theater by its architecture: the balconies, the ornate moldings, ceilings and the sloping floor front to back. But the most important advantage of converting a movie theater into a concert hall is the incredible acoustics you get.

sporting-goods shop. I still liked KISS, and when I saw *Hotter than Hell*—with an even more bizarre cover than their first—I grabbed it. I made a cassette copy of it for my new Sony boom box, which I took with me on a two-week trip to Puerto Rico in February 1975. I played *Hotter than Hell* repeatedly on the beach. That's when I knew they were for me—KISS had become my favorite band.

After I returned home, a couple of weeks passed and then I heard *Dressed to Kill* was out. It featured a simpler cover: KISS was indeed dressed to kill—wearing suits and ties along with their makeup. Bob Gruen took the cover photo on the corner of 23rd Street and Eighth Avenue in New York (his entire shoot became popular when *Creem* featured the band in a photographic comic strip). Later I got to know Bob when I became a professional photographer and we shot the same bands. Like KISS' other two albums, I quickly put *Dressed to Kill* on my stereo and cranked "C'mon and Love Me."

Picture by Susan Dayton

Playing my Walnut Gibson SG guitar on the patio at my family's estate in Upper Brookville, New York, spring 1974.

I told my brother Peter we had to see this show. Boy, did I regret not seeing KISS' debut at the Academy the year before! Since then, their shows had been getting a lot of press. The opening act at the Beacon show was Jo Jo Gunne; Peter and I decided to skip them. All the bands were doing two shows that night. KISS had sold out the first show so another concert was quickly added. My brother and I went to a seven o' clock or an eight o' clock show and I decided to take along my camera. . . .

Let me say something about photography here. At the time I was attending C.W. Post College taking photography courses. Photography was a long-time love of mine. I started out at Friends Academy when my science teacher taught me the mechanics of photography and how to develop film in a tiny darkroom the size of a closet. We used an old Speed Graphic camera at the school, and I mainly worked with 4x5 negatives. I still remember the first time I saw an image come up through the chemicals on the print. Seeing the image come to life was exciting. Later I had access to a better darkroom, which made photography more fun. When I lived in California, I had photographed Grand Funk Railroad and Rod Stewart at the L.A. Forum from the audience. They were small images, but it was fun to bring a camera to a concert without any expectations. I certainly did not intend to become a professional photographer at that time.

At college I learned when there's less-than-perfect light you could "push" the film—meaning you could increase the light sensitivity by rating the film higher. This is called increasing the ASA, now known as ISO. When I developed film, I compensated for this setting by leaving it in the developing solution longer than usual. This would make an image a little grainy but, with theatrical stage lighting, I could always get enough light to shoot an image without using a flash. I pushed ASA 400 film to 1600 to get good concert images.

The night of the KISS show I brought along a Pentax SpotMatic body with an attached lens and a Vivitar telephoto lens. I also brought only black-and-white film, not color. I loved working in black and white, not only because I learned how to develop b/w film on my own, but also because I loved the stark-contrast imagery that came up on the paper. The camera was simple—fully manual with a built-in, basic match-needle light meter. The best way to learn the ins and outs of photography is to use that kind of equipment.

Rod Stewart at the LA Forum, 1971. One of my first concert photos, developed and printed at Orange Coast College in Costa Mesa, California.

Now back to the concert . . . .

KISS exploded onto the stage with a fury I'd never seen before.

I was seated way up in the balcony, but I could still feel the bombs and hear the music loud and clear. Then I realized I could get good shots if I walked down to the brass railing edging the front of the balcony that extended all the way out to the middle of the theater. I didn't have to worry about being hustled back to my seat; security didn't really bother you much back then. I looked through the viewfinder—I had a great line on KISS. I had perfect range up there—far enough away to get the band members into one frame yet, with the telephoto, the view looked as if I was practically on top of them. That was the first time I photographed KISS, and those images are very special to me.

The KISS show at the Beacon blew me away. I couldn't get enough of them. Their stage show—with the bombs, the music and the overall energy—exhilarated me. I had to see them again and I didn't care how.

My next stop was Boston....

THE ORPHEUM

THE ORPHEUM IS another theater where the seats slope up and there's a balcony. Although KISS had three albums out and had headlined in other cities, they opened for a group called the Hunter Ronson Band in Boston. Hunter was Ian Hunter from Mott the Hoople and Ronson was the late Mick Ronson from David Bowie's Spiders from Mars. They had a great track record and some popularity, but I'm not sure if they had released an album.

Before I took off for Boston, I made a couple of enlargements from the Beacon show and mounted the 11x14s on cardboard. I thought, *Boy, I'd like to meet Paul Stanley and show him a shot.* I figured KISS would get a kick out of seeing themselves captured live. I got to the theater in the afternoon and found out where KISS was staying. At their hotel I went right up to the desk—in the old days you could actually do that—and asked which room Paul Stanley was in. Believe it or not, the clerk actually told me!

I walked onto a crowded elevator that soon stopped on the fourth floor. This guy—with long black hair and two cans of Coke—stepped in facing me (I still remember those two cans of Coke like it was yesterday). Before he could turn around, I ask, "Are you Paul Stanley?" and he says, "Yeah." I say, "My name is Chip and I'm from New York. I have a photo of you. Can I show it to you?" He says, "Sure, come with me." We walk down the hall together.

When we get to his room Paul puts his sodas down and looks at the photo. "That was the Beacon Theater two months ago," I say. Paul says the photo is great. Then he yells, "Hey, Peter! There's a guy named Chip here from New York who has pictures of us from the Beacon!"

Peter Criss steps out of the bathroom—shirtless and combing his hair (just out of the shower, I guess)—and says, "Hey, that's cool, man." I notice Peter seems a little older than Paul does. I shake his hand while Paul goes through the regalia laid out on the bed. He turns the photo over and exclaims "CHIP ROCK!!" I explain that Chip is my nickname (I added "Rock" in college when I was writing for the school paper and kept it when I moved on to photography). Paul asks me if I am going to the show that night, and I tell him I am. We talk about ten to fifteen minutes, then Paul says they need to take a nap before the show. I had planned to meet my brother Peter and his friends from college, so I actually had to go anyway. I excused myself and left the hotel, thinking that Paul was impressed that I'd traveled all the way from New York to see KISS.

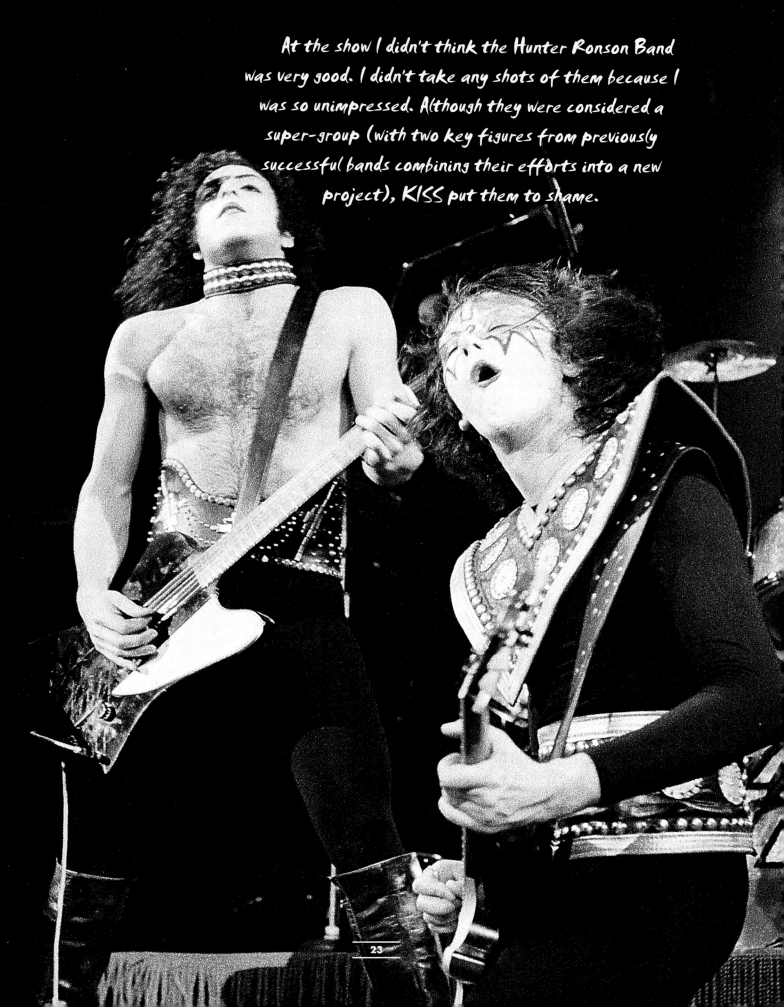

At the show I didn't think the Hunter Ronson Band was very good. I didn't take any shots of them because I was so unimpressed. Although they were considered a super-group (with two key figures from previously successful bands combining their efforts into a new project), KISS put them to shame.

This photo is the actual shot I showed Paul Stanley and Peter Criss in their hotel room in Boston, 1975. Right is an unpublished outtake.

When KISS came on, Paul apologized to the audience for not using any of their signature pyrotechnics. "The Boston Fire Department won't let us to use any of our *special effects*," with "special effects" enunciated viciously. To be honest, the audience didn't react to KISS; they were mostly a Hunter Ronson Band crowd—their loss.

That trip was an all-around success. I had another opportunity to photograph this amazing rock group and I met a couple of the band members, too. Back then, however, I never really considered photographing these early concerts as a springboard for shooting rock bands for a living. I got a charge out of seeing my work, showing it to the bands and impressing them. Back then there were no regulations about cameras or anything. You could usually bring in your equipment without any hassles.

There were times backstage when KISS fans would come up to them and show them not-so-good pictures they'd taken with their point-and-shoot 110 cameras. Gene Simmons would make a point to tell them how good their shots were, but I knew I was getting a sincere response when he would see my 16x20s of him spewing flame above his head. Compliments from KISS were my driving force for shooting them as enthusiastically as I did.

It was almost unbelievable—Paul really is a rock star with his long, black mane and his flashy clothes.

KISS played the Orpheum again about a year later, and I had an interesting experience that always sticks in my mind: I was hanging in front of their hotel when Paul comes out to enter his limousine. He invites me to come to soundcheck and—believe it or not—I foolishly declined! Why? I said that I needed to change clothes before going to the show. Paul—looking at me strangely—says "Okay" and left! After the limousine sped out of the lot I wanted to kick myself—I really could have skipped changing for the show for this once-in-a-lifetime opportunity. At the arena, Paul stops me and says, "You should have come to soundcheck—we did 'Room Service'!" To this day I regret not going to that soundcheck.

THE CALDERONE

THE THIRD TIME I photographed KISS was at the Calderone Concert Hall in Hempstead, New York, which was close to where I lived at the time. Now, it wasn't the real old kind of venue that I previously described, but was more of a 1950s or 1960s movie theater that held a couple of thousand people. I don't think it had a balcony, but I was up on a slope and I had a good spot. This was where I made a connection with some family members of KISS, which led to my knowing the band personally.

I brought my best shots and printed them big for impact. To make a great impression, you have to have a good photo blown up to 16x20 or 20x24. There was some grain in the prints because I enlarged them so much, but that only added more character and a certain roughness to them. Included in this batch were great shots of Gene with smoke around him at the Orpheum enlarged to 16x20 on Agfa paper, and some of Paul at the Beacon Theater.

I had parked my car in the theater lot when I saw this older couple walking by. I had a feeling that they were related to somebody in KISS. I asked them if they were parents of one of the members of the band. The man said, "How did you know? We're Paul Stanley's parents." Well, I pulled out a print of Paul, introduced myself and showed them my photo of their son.

The Eisens really liked it. Mr. Eisen asked if I would sell it, so I suggested twenty bucks. I was honored that someone from KISS' family was impressed enough to buy my work. I'll always remember them walking off into the darkness holding one of my photos. Later I found out the Eisens have my photo framed and hanging on a wall in their home.

Once inside the theater, I overheard someone talking about going backstage. I joined the crowd around her and—can you believe this—she said, "I'm Lydia Criss, Peter Criss' wife." I showed her my picture of Gene and she asked if she could take it backstage. I gladly handed the print to her, then she disappeared into the theater and I heard nothing else about it.

For the Calderone show, I had borrowed a Canon F1—a top-of-the-line 35mm camera—from my college's photo department. That kind of camera was out of my financial reach. Fortunately, Canon had a lender program with college photography departments that provided cameras to students in hopes of encouraging a brand loyalty after they graduated.

This was also the first time I shot the band in color, using Kodak's Tungsten film. It's balanced for artificial light and renders it without the yellow haze you get with daylight film. I also pushed the film to increase the speed, which again made for more grain in the prints. These pictures turned out great.

THE TOWER THEATER AND CAPITOL THEATER

WHEN I HEARD that KISS was going to play the Tower Theater in Philadelphia and the Capitol Theater in New Jersey one night after the other, I got in my car and drove to Philadelphia. I had made up some 8x10s to sell on the street. I did not intend to circumnavigate KISS' licensing, I just wanted to make some money to offset my travel costs and supplies. The most expensive aspect of my photography was paper and film, since I could get away with developing and printing shots at my school.

After the show, I went across the street because you weren't allowed to sell at the exits. I was holding up a photograph and yelling, "For sale, two dollars!" when my first customers—a distinguished older gentleman and

Here is Billy Squire's first group Piper, pictured with KISS manager Bill Aucoin and Sean Delaney.

his wife looking rather incongruous in the crowd of young people—came up to me, looked at my photos and said, "I'll take two." I sold maybe ten or twenty more shots and made fifty dollars to pay for gas and food. That night, I slept in my car somewhere in New Jersey. The next day, I stopped at an old beachfront hotel in Atlantic City to kill some time, then headed for the Capitol Theater.

I got lucky that next night—I met Gene Simmons. I also met two members of another band that KISS' management handled called Starz, Richie Ranno and Brenden Harkin. Brenden invited me backstage. Once there, I ask where KISS is and someone actually tells me! What are the chances of that happening today?

I knock on the dressing room door and say I'm a photographer who wants to show Gene Simmons a photo. Sure enough, I'm in! In this tiny room Gene's putting on the final touches of his makeup. I notice this room is not very well lit, and KISS relies on the lights from their vanity mirrors to see what they are doing. I shove the photo in front of him. He says, "Wow—you took this?"

After nodding anxiously, Gene tells me he already has the same photo in his apartment—it's the print I gave to Lydia Criss at the Calderone! He asks if I'm shooting the show tonight, and I tell him I am. He explained that he had to finish putting on his makeup, so I left Gene's dressing room to find a place to shoot the show.

This is the photo that Gene Simmons signed for me the first time I met him. It's also the shot that Lydia Criss gave him some months earlier.

PORT HURON

IT WAS NOW late 1975. I loved photographing KISS and I was gratified that they liked my work. Waiting for them to come back to New York wasn't enough for me. When I had first met Paul he encouraged me to go up to their management office to see if they would buy my photos. "Why not?" I thought.

Aucoin Management worked out of Glickman/Marks' advertising agency on Madison Avenue in midtown New York City. Their art director was Dennis Woloch. I later developed a relationship with Dennis on various projects, including *The Originals* album booklet, the first concert program, and later with *Alive II* in 1977. Back then you could just call up the office and ask for a KISS tour itinerary. They were touring constantly at this point. Aucoin's office told me the band was heading west, stopping in Michigan and southern Canada first. This was the first time I would travel a great distance to see the band.

At this point, I was working odd jobs to support myself. I didn't require all that much, just some spending money and a car. A car was not only transportation—it could be lodging when necessary. I could always find money to see KISS. This time I scraped up enough to get a plane ticket.

I flew to Michigan without any planning or clearance from Aucoin Management, mostly because I didn't know how to obtain photo passes then. All I'd done up to that point was show up with my equipment and shoot.

I arrived at Detroit airport without a credit card, so I had to beg for a car rental. I drove to Port Huron, which took about two hours. The McMoran Place Arena was an old rundown Midwestern hockey rink probably built in the 1940s. I found the gate where KISS would enter the arena. I was hanging out when a security guard came up to me and said, "Get outta here!" I moved about twenty-feet away—I didn't intend to actually leave. The gate opened when he wasn't looking, so I walked inside. Unfortunately, he caught me a little while later. He said if I didn't leave, he'd make sure I didn't see the show that night!

Just then, a limousine pulls up. It's like a movie—the limousine charges up and the driver throws on the brakes. Dust swirls as the vehicle stops at the gate entrance. Paul jumps out and runs up the steps. When he sees me, he takes me by the arm and leads me right inside! I didn't plan it that way, but it is such a thrill for Paul to recognize me and treat me like one of the family. I felt like a million bucks just passing by that security guard with the bad attitude.

Paul continues up the stairs to the back of the stage and I stay at the bottom. I see him grab a Flying V and disappear behind the amps to the front of the stage. The next thing I hear is the crunch of the guitar: "WRRREHHHH!" To see someone go somewhere he's never been before and take it over like his own backyard—so cool.

After soundcheck, I ask Paul if I can get a photo pass for the show so I can shoot in the pit. In no time their top security guy is slapping a pass on my denim jacket!

Later that night after donning my official KISS pass, I head for the arena. I hung out and watched the crew finish setting up the stage. Guess which security guard apologized for being such a jerk that afternoon? I was in such a good mood there were no bad vibes in me at all.

I had photo clearance for the first time, but I didn't go in the photo pit for the first song. Instead I did something that has been my style ever since: I went to the soundboard, introduced myself to the soundman, showed him my pass and asked him if I could photograph from there.

He agreed. The angle from there is so good and the sound is incredible. The soundboard is also raised above the audience's heads, so there's no chance of losing a great shot because someone got in front of me at a crucial moment. I stayed at the soundboard for the first five songs, then went into the pit for the first time as an official KISS photographer with a 20mm extreme wide-angle lens.

KISS shows were as exciting for me as they were for the fans. Sometimes my enthusiasm surprised the crew. They were so involved with getting the pyrotechnics and lights right each night, they could be pretty blasé about the show in general. But I was enthusiastic with every gig.

TRAVERSE CITY

THE TRAVERSE CITY concert was the KISS show that never was. Traverse City is in the northernmost part of Michigan, about one hundred-sixty miles from Port Huron. The local radio was publicizing the show and Bob Seger, a Michigan native, was opening, so it was a big event for a relatively small town. The arena, which was really a hockey rink, was completely packed with kids. I had met the soundman the night before so, true to my new style, I asked if I could shoot from the board again.

KISS never performed that night because of some electrical problem that couldn't be fixed. Bob Seger's set was okay but, right after he was finished, something went wrong. As the crew brought down the lights, KISS quickly and quietly left the arena in their makeup and costumes! The fans were angry and the guards had their hands full trying to keep them from getting violent. Those around KISS tried to protect them from any furor that might break out.

Situations like this have led to riots and worse, but there wasn't any danger that night. Just as KISS hurried into their limousines, an announcement was made that the band couldn't play. There was a lot of booing and someone threw a bottle on stage, and that was about it for the show that never was.

I was as sad as anyone else could be. With a sideways stage and a close soundboard, I would have made some remarkable shots that night with my telephoto lens. I never had an opportunity like that again. The mood in Traverse City was flat-out dejection; everyone was bummed out.

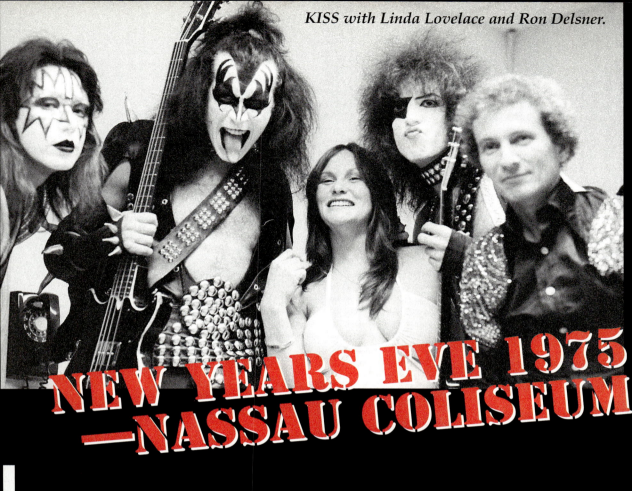

KISS with Linda Lovelace and Ron Delsner.

NEW YEARS EVE 1975 —NASSAU COLISEUM

IT WAS THE end of 1975. In the course of nine months, I had shot KISS about five or six times. I met some people at the Aucoin office and had submitted some photos. They seemed impressed with my work. I especially noticed KISS' popularity among my friends, who at first had no clue what band I was shooting. They were saying they'd heard KISS a lot on the radio.

Alive! was out and had hit the Top 10. The live versions of "Strutter" and "Rock and Roll All Nite" were getting a lot of air play in the New York area and it looked like they were finally going to make it big-time. They were selling out big arenas and were planning their first concert programs. In each city where KISS toured there were more established and better-equipped photographers on the guest list. But I had shot some good stuff, so the band believed in me.

KISS was now back in their hometown for one of the most exciting holidays of the year. The last time they played New Year's Eve in New York, they were among three bands opening up for Blue Oyster Cult at the Academy of Music, which held only a few thousand people. Now, only two years later to the day, they were headlining Nassau Coliseum with a capacity of about sixteen-thousand people—and Blue Oyster Cult was second on the bill! Leslie West of Mountain came on first. His drummer was Carmine Appice, an original member of Vanilla Fudge who later worked with Rod Stewart for many years. Eventually, Carmine would work with Paul Stanley on his solo album.

It was this show where I met Fin Costello, with whom I got along well over the years. Fin shot the cover of *Alive!* It is interesting that this was actually staged during a soundcheck. This was the same show that Linda Lovelace, a porn star known for her film *Deep Throat*, met KISS for the first time. I took a photo of them

This is the cover shot of KISS' first-ever tour program, 1976.

shot from the crowd with my new 28mm angle lens, but I was being jostled. It was [festi]val seating, which means that everyone was [crowd]ing wherever they could. The place was [fille]d to the rafters with screaming fans.

together backstage that was printed in many rock magazines.

By now, I knew all the ins and outs of getting passes for shows, and I got a photo pass for the Nassau show with no problem. It was the first big concert I was able to photograph officially with all the perks that go with it. I was led to the backstage area with other members of the press. Because I was assigned to shoot the upcoming tour program, the management wanted me to have the best-possible photo advantage. Time and quality were of the essence. Bill Aucoin specifically said he wanted all the shots in color that night, not my accustomed black and white. I did what he said, but I felt I could capture KISS best in black and white. Black and silver are the colors in black-and-white film—the black of their leather and the silver of their costumes. But I was comfortable with both formats.

Bill also wanted me to shoot with slide film instead of print. The main difference between shooting print and transparency is the ability of the film to compensate for over or under exposure when printing. Print film has incredible latitude, color transparency film has practically none—if you miscalculate the exposure, you're stuck with that image.

The soundboard was too far away that night to be an option; besides, I loved shooting from the audience because no one else bothered to make the effort. I love getting shots where people's arms are in the image, enhancing the main subject. It's like an audience-eye view. I decided to get an overhead shot—that's when you hold the camera above your head and shoot without looking in the viewfinder—and shot a whole sequence that came out perfect. (This included a great shot of Gene breathing fire that made it into *KISStory*.) Around this time bands were decreeing a three-song limit to photographers, though I was given carte blanche to shoot anytime and anywhere I wanted.

These shots came out great. I was very proud of them. I asked Bill Aucoin if I could

present my slides instead of just handing over the work. It would be far more dramatic to see the pictures projected up on a wall. KISS' popularity was so big by then that Aucoin had moved from a cramped room in Glickman/Marks' advertising agency to a beautiful office on Madison Avenue. The conference room had leather chairs, a huge circular table and state-of-the-art stereo equipment.

The next day I walked into 645 Madison Avenue lugging a projector and my parents' old movie screen. My equipment wasn't impressive—the screen had a rip on the bottom—but it would serve its purpose. When Bill Aucoin saw I was serious about using a screen, he let me finish setting up.

As we went through the slides, Bill wouldn't stop and discuss them. All he said was, "Next, next, next. . . ."

Suddenly this certain picture flashed on the screen—one of those overhead shots (it was actually underexposed!). I had intended to get an overall picture with all the lights, but spots of different colors were on each band member. The photo came out pure black with these beautiful, dramatic colors around the band. They looked somewhat small in the center of the stage because I had used my wide-angle lens and I was about fifty feet away in the audience, but the photo was crystal clear.

Bill Aucoin—I swear to God—actually leaped out of his chair to look at the screen. He didn't say anything, he just looked at the shot. Then he sat back and continued saying, "Next,

next, next. . . ." At least I knew he liked one shot. I left the office feeling satisfied, thinking I would get a credit for a photo or two in KISS' concert program.

A couple of weeks went by and I didn't hear anything, so I decided to give Dennis Woloch a call. He said, "Yeah, you got the cover," somewhat nonchalantly. I almost dropped the telephone. I had gotten the cover of the first-ever KISS concert program! I was floored. Then Dennis said, "And you got a some full-pagers and a couple of other shots. Don't worry, you're in there." It wasn't a big deal to him because I was just one of several other photographers involved in the project, but it was monumental to me. I was only paid about twenty bucks a shot and given a fifty-dollar bonus for the cover, but it was a feather in my cap. It was my first real money in rock photography.

The program would go on sale for the first time at Detroit's Cobo Hall arena in January 1976. KISS had managed to sell out three nights in a fifteen-thousand-seat arena. It was going to be the pinnacle—so far—of their career.

It was back to Detroit and on to Cobo Hall for me.

Fan with Paul's guitar neck after the Nassau concert in the first minutes of 1976.

COBO HALL
JANUARY 1976

HAVING MATERIAL IN the first-ever KISS tour program meant a lot to me, so I wanted to go to Detroit for its unveiling. This was my first major piece of published work and, like an artist showing his work in a gallery, I had to be present for its premiere. There was going to be a one-night show in Chester, Pennsylvania, and the management gave me permission to go there and then on to Cobo Hall.

My brother Peter was happy to come with me. We piled into my Volkswagen 411 and decided to bring along my golden retriever, Trevor. At ten o'clock that morning it was bitterly cold and starting to snow in New York. By three o'clock that afternoon, we had to drive four more hours to Chester. There was no way we going to make it on time. I had no way of contacting the band or management, so we slept in the freezing car that night. (I swear Trevor kept us alive—the only warmth we had was coming off his body!) In the early morning I turned up the heater full blast and headed for Detroit.

KISS was staying in some fancy old hotel we couldn't afford. We ended up getting a room in a dilapidated downtown hotel that didn't even care we were walking through the lobby with a dog behind us. We left Trevor at the hotel and headed for Cobo Hall.

There was slush everywhere and my feet were soaked. When we got to the arena we discovered there wasn't a guest list. The head of security let us in to get out of the snow. There was a huge group of fans waiting in the cold for KISS to arrive. In those days, seeing KISS without their makeup was a big deal. There were so many people the limousines couldn't get close enough to the building for the band to get out and enter the arena. Finally, one limousine got close to the backstage door and Peter ducked out while the security guards shielded his face with their leather-covered hands.

When Bill Aucoin saw me backstage he asked, "Weren't you supposed to be in Pennsylvania last night?" as if he were annoyed

Ace "smoking" at Springfield, MA.

that someone had put my name on the guest list and then I didn't show up. I told him we fell behind schedule and he seemed to understand.

There was a lot of excitement in the air for the concert, but the greatest anticipation for me was seeing the concert program. I knew I had the cover, but I didn't know what it was going to look like in print. In the merchandising area of the arena, there was a stack of programs about head-high—hundreds and hundreds of them. The merchandising guy was distributing the programs to the vendors. I said, "Hi, my name is Chip Rock. I've got some photos in here and I'd like to take a couple programs." He told me to take as many as I wanted. I only took about five. (If I had taken a hundred and locked them up in a vault, I'd be a rich man now!) I have only one of those programs left, and it's frayed and falling apart.

The program I drove almost six hundred miles to get was now in my hands. When I started looking through it, I was blown away. Besides the cover, I had a full-page shot of Gene from the Calderone, a full-page shot of Peter from Boston and various other shots—and I had credits on all of them! I thought Dennis Woloch had done a great job putting the booklet together.

Alan Miller, who was Bill Aucoin's assistant, started inviting photographers backstage. I was afraid I wasn't "official" enough to be invited. Many photographers with lots of equipment acted like they owned the place. When I hesitated, Alan turned to me and said, "Okay, Chip, go ahead!" At that moment, I really felt like I belonged. What a great feeling!

Once there, I see Ace Frehley tuning his guitar in full makeup and costume. I heard that Ace is fussy about his tuning, so I decide to save a formal introduction for another time—I go over and sit next to him without speaking. Soon the band had only ten minutes before they went on—and Ace was still tuning his guitars! When he finished, a roadie tied a white towel around the neck so nothing would touch the strings.

When they opened the door at six o'clock, the place was flooded with fans. This wasn't

KISS' first visit to Cobo Hall—that famous audience shot of two fans holding up a banner on the back cover of *Alive!* was taken at this arena—so this crowd knew exactly what they were in for.

Local TV crews were lined up outside. KISS also hired a crew to professionally shoot the show. Years later I saw the final edited video that was released to the bootleg market. Unfortunately it doesn't translate the excitement of actually being there.

There seemed to be a commotion in the next room. It looked surreal: a group of middle-aged men in suits mingling with the press and fans. Looming over their heads were four six-foot, seven-inch tall men in black leather and makeup. KISS was getting the keys to the City of Detroit.

Just before the show started, Bill told me Waring Abbott would shoot that night's show from the pit, but I was welcome to shoot from the audience. I was allowed in the photo pit on the second night, which was fine with me. Waring was more established, and I was happy to be one of the only two photographers allowed to shoot the show at all.

My brother and I watched KISS perform on the first night. The second night was mine to shoot. In the pit I had to crouch down a lot so my head wouldn't obstruct the view of fans behind me. Even crouched down, I still got a great shot of Gene breathing fire (which appears in *KISStory*).

My brother and I weren't able to sleep in the hotel that night; the expenses were mounting and we were running out of funds for the ride home. Although we had to leave, both KISS shows had been fabulous, and I was happy I had covered the band photographically as well as possible.

KISS is presented with a key to Detroit Rock City, 1976.

CANADA, 1976

AFTER **COBO HALL** in January 1976, the tour continued into the spring. The band was scheduled to play dates in March on successive nights in Kitchener and in London, Canada. Those places were within striking distance of my house. Another trip to see KISS—would it be worth it? Although I didn't have a photo pass this time, you bet it was worth it. I decided to drive there alone.

At the band's hotel in London, I asked Gene if he wanted to look at some shots. Gene said something that made me proud. You know when you look back on something really special and think, "No one can take that away from me"? That's how I feel about that moment. After looking over my photos, Gene turned to me and said, "You're our biggest fan." I'm sure Gene has told other people that through the years, but it was one of the greatest days in my life. Even to

this day when KISS is playing and Gene's voice hits me, I think of that moment.

Fortunately, I landed a photo pass for both shows anyway. Since I was the only photographer from New York, I had great access. The London and Kitchener shows were medium-sized with about a six-thousand-seat capacity. The only other person sharing the pit with me was the local news photographer, and he was only going to be there for the first couple of songs. At the Kitchener show the stage was incredibly low, only two or three feet off the ground. I got one of my best "Black Diamond" shots from this show because I stood up briefly when KISS got into formation.

Back in Gene's hotel room, I noticed he had some incredibly weird jewelry—skull rings, eyeball rings, a spider bracelet and assorted chain necklaces and belts. I thought it would be a great idea to get some shots of Gene's jewelry and paraphernalia, but Paul had a frown on his face when he heard about that. It was obvious he didn't like the idea. When I got to Gene's room with my

gear, Paul had told Gene that he didn't think it was a good idea for Gene to have his jewelry photographed, especially if this was going to be for publication. I felt badly that these photos didn't work out, especially because I found out later that they let Bob Gruen shoot the jewelry for *Playboy*.

To this day I have always had a great relationship with the members of KISS. In the 1970s, they were rock stars who didn't have to answer to anyone. When they were joking around and included me, it made me feel like part of the family.

One such instance happened after I'd photographed a show in Springfield, Massachusetts. I was sitting with my brother at breakfast when Paul walked in with his security guard. He really stood out with his long hair, though no one else seemed to take notice of him. We had no intentions of going over and bothering him; but as we started to walk out, Paul jumped up from his chair and interrupted his breakfast to come over and say hi to me and meet my brother. These kinds of considerate things warmed my heart.

Warring Abbott photographing Paul Stanley backstage while I'm photographing them, Cobo Hall, 1976

Kiss with promoter Steve Glantz.

MIAMI, FLORIDA

THE MIAMI FRONTON show was particularly memorable for me because it revisited me almost fifteen years later. By the late 1970s, I was shooting a bunch of different rock bands—Cheap Trick, Heart, Van Halen, ELO and the New York Dolls. I had work published in the inner sleeve of the Ramones' *Road to Ruin* LP and I did the first tour program for the Cars. But KISS was my main priority—anytime there was a KISS-related event, I wanted to be involved.

At that time, there was a foldout magazine named *Poster Press* that promoted one band each issue. While there was some text, its main draw was it opened up to a full-sized poster. *Poster Press* was created by Bob Guccione, Jr., publisher of *Spin* and son of the famous publisher of *Penthouse* magazine.

When I saw that one issue was going to feature KISS, I called the head offices—which were actually in the *Penthouse* offices—to offer some of my shots. I met Bob Guccione, Jr. and he looked at my stuff. He seemed impressed with my portfolio and mentioned he needed a cover for the KISS issue.

I was excited about this project. When I told Bill Aucoin about it, he just shrugged and walked away. I should have known something was up; KISS nixed the project before it even took off.

The Miami Jai Alai Fronton show turned out to be a great venue for camera angles. The opening act was .38 Special, Donnie Van Zant's band. The sloping floor offered great shots no matter where I stood. The first song was "Deuce," which I shot from the audience. I got a great color shot with my telephoto lens that I kept in my archives, since I wasn't going to be submitting it to Guccione for his magazine.

Sixteen years later *USA Today* called me when KISS' *Revenge* album came out. They wanted a group action shot from the makeup days to go with an article was about the new generation of fans into KISS. The publication date was Tuesday, June 22, 1993, and the heading was "A New Generation of Rock Fans Fall in Love with KISS." I used the shot from the Miami Fronton show because it captured the feeling of that era.

This is the first photo that Ace signed for me.

DESTROYER DRESS REHEARSAL

WHILE KISS WAS touring in Canada, *Destroyer* was released. The band was still using their *Alive!* outfits because there had been no time to make new ones (although incomplete prototypes were used for one photo session the band held while recording "Great Expectations" in New York). KISS was planning a new American tour that summer with new costumes and staging.

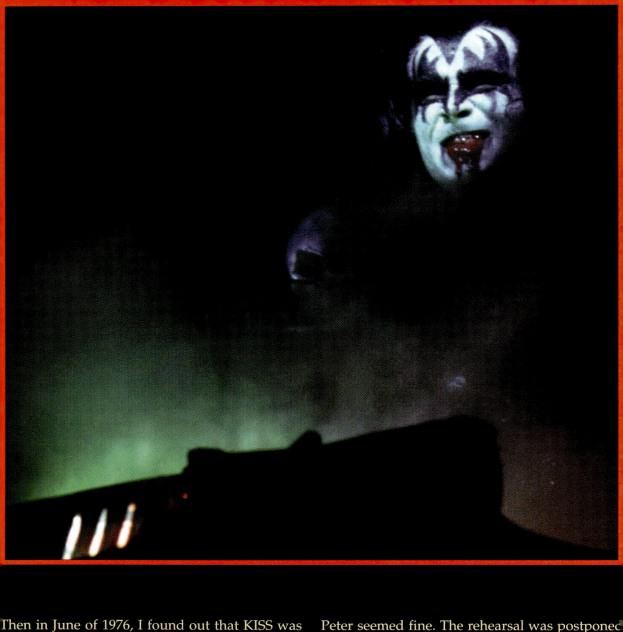

Then in June of 1976, I found out that KISS was dress rehearsing with their new costumes and staging in an airplane hangar at Stewart Air Force Base in Newburgh, New York. Certain members of the media were invited and I was one of them!

A story in *The New York Times* had caught my eye: "KISS drummer injured in car accident." Evidently Peter Criss and Paul Chavarria had been driving on the runway at the Air Force base in a Mercedes when the car hit something and flipped over. I asked someone about it at the dress rehearsal, but no one made a big deal about it.

Peter seemed fine. The rehearsal was postponed for one day, but I never found out if it was because of the accident.

Alan Miller told me that I didn't have to drive up for the rehearsal; they would bring me in a limousine. This ended up being a mistake because they insisted we go to this elaborate luncheon first and the damned thing went on until four-thirty in the afternoon. I could have been at the hangar getting ready.

When we got to the base KISS was already there—dressed in their new outfits. Paul had this black, skin-tight costume with sequins all over it

Ace playing a rarely used Gibson Explorer at the Destroyer rehearsal in Newburgh, NY.

Ace wore an outfit with a spacey-looking, triangular front piece and Peter was in a black-and-silver jumpsuit. Gene had created his signature gargoyle suit to match a prop, like an old twisted tree from a horror movie.

The stage was at least eight or ten feet high and I couldn't get a good angle. There was hardly any room to move because the carpenters hadn't cleared the area. All the tables and saws were still under the stage from its construction.

Finally, the lights went down and they started to play. It was a little ragged, but I was just shooting away. I bumped into another photographer and he shoved me out of the way—pretty rude! Then there was the debris. I kept having to dodge 2x4s and saws to keep from tripping. After the rehearsal, the band came to greet us and then walked outside to meet fans that had gotten wind of this secret event.

It was at this time I met and spoke with Ace for the first time. I had intentionally brought along a 20x24 print of Ace with his smoking guitar that I'd shot in Springfield, Massachusetts. It was a dramatic black-and-white shot. After the band finished their performance I introduced myself and showed him the photo. He just said, "Wow!" so I handed it to him. Then Alan Miller stormed in and said, "Chip, this is not the time for this. The limousines are waiting and we have to get back to New York!" I didn't want the limos to begin with—I wanted to take my own car and not be at anyone else's mercy. I had no choice; I could see my opportunity to talk to Ace slipping away.

Me in the "guitar room" after a show with confetti in my hair.

There was another time I met up with Ace. I asked if I could show him some photos and we went back to his room. He started flipping through my portfolio when suddenly he stopped at one photo and yelled, "THAT guitar was stolen!" He slammed the book shut and stormed out of the room.

THE DESTROYER TOUR

DESTROYER WAS OUT and the tour hit the road with a new stage, new costumes and new effects. The first show was at the Scope Arena in Norfolk, Virginia, with Bob Seger opening for KISS.

I was intent on going to the first night of the tour. I took the train down to Norfolk and rented a car to get to the show. At this point Barry Levine had come on the scene and had virtually become KISS' number-one photographer. I asked Alan Miller if I could go to the concert and told him I would stay out of the pit and just shoot from the audience. Alan talked to Barry, who grudgingly agreed to it. Despite that, I still got some great shots.

The next KISS show I photographed took place in Toledo, Ohio, and was the first time I was actually paid by management for an entire live shoot. I was promised two hundred bucks, but my plane ticket cost me more than that. The concert, however, was still a success: Bill Aucoin had asked me to arrange a group shot of KISS with the members of Starz. I had bought brand-new flash equipment but couldn't afford a battery pack. I went to a hardware store in Toledo and bought six extension cords to hook up the flash. The guys from KISS and Starz, along with Aucoin and the promoters, waited patiently while I ran a one hundred twenty-foot extension to my flash. They playfully said to me, "C'mon, Chip—the show must go on!" I did get the shot and it ended up being published—*Music Life* in Japan was the first to print it.

Jersey City, July 1976.

I always found KISS fans to be great people. Some of them would recognize my name from photo credits in magazines, the first tour program or the *Originals* booklet. When I'd shoot from the audience, they'd give me elbowroom, steady my legs or hold me up so I could get a shot. I always made it a point to get along with the fans—after all, I'm one, too.

Sometimes you can't win. Let me tell you how my idea of Gene's advice backfired on me. One day in New York I ran into Gene at the Aucoin office. I was wearing frayed, cut-off jeans with a ropy belt—kind of a hippie look—along with sandals or sneakers and no socks. He whispered, "I have something to tell you," and I thought he was going to tell me that I was the best KISS photographer ever or that I was his biggest fan or something like that, so my ears perked up.

I was crushed when he said, "You're not dressed properly for business. When I do business, I dress up. You can't expect to do business looking that way." I decided to put his advice into action on my future visits to KISS'

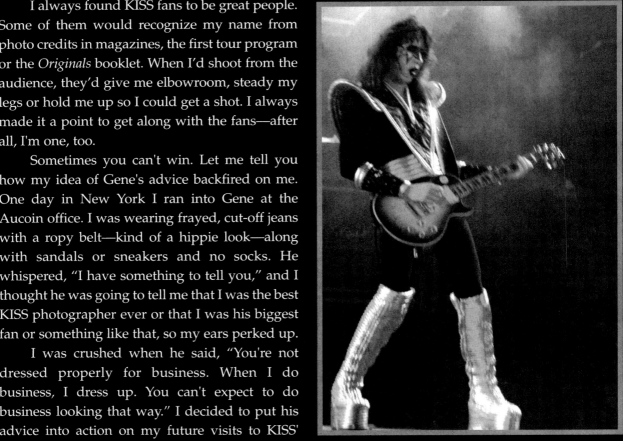

management offices. A few months later I had arranged a slide show for a band named Siren—which later became Spyder. I bought a tan suit with a vest, a white shirt, muted red tie with little dots on it and leather shoes. This was my interpretation of Gene's advice to "dress up for business." Bill Aucoin took one look at me and said, "Boy, these must be *really* good pictures!" No one else was dressed up for the meeting, and I felt totally out of place. I guess I misinterpreted Gene's dress code!

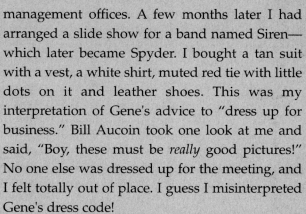

July 31, Toledo, OH

Cape Cod, MA.

New Haven, CT.

IN THE SUMMER of '77, I went back to Canada because KISS was playing London and Kitchener again. You'd think Canada would be cooler than New York in the summer, but it must have been one hundred degrees there—overcast and stifling.

At the Kitchener Arena, Ace, Paul and I were hanging out near the venue. They weren't wearing their makeup and it made me feel trusted because, in those days, photographers were offered big bucks to take a picture of KISS without their makeup on. That meant a lot to me.

The stage was only about two feet off the floor, a great angle for me, and I had the pit to myself for the whole show—the best photo opportunity I ever had! The next day we were off to London, a couple of hours from Toronto.

When we arrived at the hotel, I met Gene and Paul in the lobby and Gene looked at me and asked, "Okay, How'd did you get here *this* time?" We laughed as I noticed that Gene was carrying an entire video equipment box complete with video camera, videocassette player and accessories.

Gene and I went up to his room, where he started to fidget around with the television for a few moments. Soon he began to play some videotapes which were, shall we say, of a "personal nature." While we were watching Gene's explicit home movies with various women he had met on tour, I had asked him what city the footage was shot in.

Gene just looked at me and said, "Who *cares* what city it was shot in? Are you not seeing what's on the TV?!"

Gene with tour manager Fritz Postlethwaite.

KISS road crew with bare-chested guitar tech Paul Chavarria, 1977.

At the end of most KISS shows, the house lights would go on and the roadies would start to tear down the set. Gene and Ace would always throw out picks to the audience and the kids would be scrambling around grabbing them. I usually picked up a lot in the pit. I collected some and gave others away to my friends. I didn't think much of collecting guitar picks then and I don't think I own any now.

I went up to the barricade and Paul was smashing his guitar. I noticed the neck of the guitar fell into the photo pit. There were no photographers and it was just lying there on the floor. The stage lights were going down and some fans were going crazy trying to reach it, but the guard kept pushing them back. I decided what the heck, gained access with my pass and grabbed the neck of the guitar. It was a first for me—after years of watching this thing fly over my head, I had it in my hands!

Madison Square Garden, July 1979.

AFTER *DYNASTY CAME* out, KISS was headlining New York again back on their home ground. The tour was called "The Return of KISS." They had changed their costumes again: Ace wore a huge cape and Gene had shiny silver armor all over his body, a kind of red, ripped cape and boots with teeth on them.

I had a photo pass for the Garden. By this point I had changed my photo style; I was using Kodachrome slide film with flash. Up until this point, I had shot KISS mostly with available light. That resulted in a different look.

Even after so many years, I always felt a rush just before KISS went on stage. It was that great thrill of standing with the band backstage just before they went on.

There was tremendous excitement pulsing through the Garden with twenty-thousand fans screaming and stomping. The whole place was shaking with anticipation. What a great feeling! Then BOOM! The explosions were awesome. The band rose from underneath the stage. Spotlights flashed down on them and they started playing "King of the Night Time World." The whole place was electric!

I got into the photo pit. I could see the look of envy on fans' faces and was barraged with "How did *you* get to do this?", "How come *you* get to go closer?" and, "Have *you* seen them without the makeup?" To me, Gene, Paul, Ace and Peter were friends. But to the fans surrounding me, they were gods.

During this time I expanded my repertoire and began shooting other bands. If you were a professional photographer based in New York City, you shot the Academy of Music, Madison Square Garden or Radio City Music Hall. Invariably I'd run into Gene or Paul. Even with their wild hair and leather jackets, they'd blend in with the crowd. Few fans would recognize them without their makeup. They liked doing that.

One night Iggy Pop was playing and I bumped into Gene. I socialized with him for a while. I saw him later at the end of the show crowded within a bunch of people. I said "Gene!" and he shushed me, obviously not wanting to cause a commotion by being recognized.

This is one of several "lost" Dynasty-era shots not developed until 1998. The "effect" you see on the bottom left is actually mold.

...y friend James Holmes, backstage ...th Gene and Ace, 1979.

Regularly, fans would see a bunch of picks in the pit and beg me, "Please get me a pick! Please!" A couple of times I wouldn't dive for picks because it started to get ridiculous. Then one night a fan whipped out five dollars. At first, I'd get a pick for someone and not accept money. Later I took cash, because I wasn't compensated for expenses when I shot KISS and money could get very tight.

THE DEBUT OF ERIC CARR

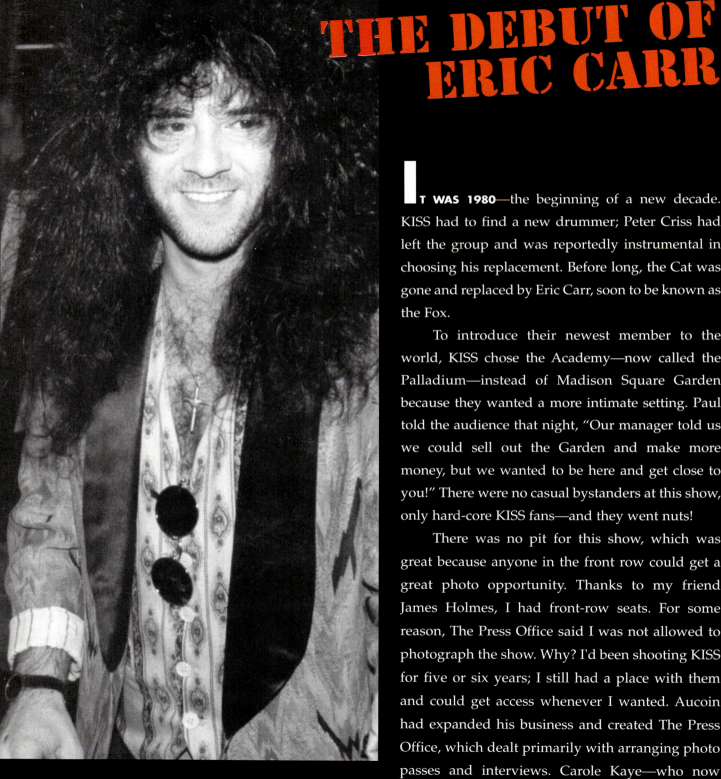

IT WAS 1980—the beginning of a new decade. KISS had to find a new drummer; Peter Criss had left the group and was reportedly instrumental in choosing his replacement. Before long, the Cat was gone and replaced by Eric Carr, soon to be known as the Fox.

To introduce their newest member to the world, KISS chose the Academy—now called the Palladium—instead of Madison Square Garden because they wanted a more intimate setting. Paul told the audience that night, "Our manager told us we could sell out the Garden and make more money, but we wanted to be here and get close to you!" There were no casual bystanders at this show, only hard-core KISS fans—and they went nuts!

There was no pit for this show, which was great because anyone in the front row could get a great photo opportunity. Thanks to my friend James Holmes, I had front-row seats. For some reason, The Press Office said I was not allowed to photograph the show. Why? I'd been shooting KISS for five or six years; I still had a place with them and could get access whenever I wanted. Aucoin had expanded his business and created The Press Office, which dealt primarily with arranging photo passes and interviews. Carole Kaye—who now

Eric's debut at the Palladium, July 1980

> Ah, the women. KISS never had a shortage of them when they were on tour and there were always enough to go around. I wasn't married then and we all had a good time.

Gene, new guitarist Vinnie Vincent, and Paul on KISS' "battle-tank" stage, 1983.

PALM BEACH, FLORIDA

MANY PEOPLE ASK me why there is such a gap in the years I had photographed KISS. The simple reason is that after the Eric Carr debut performance, I lost interest. Then I moved away from New York City and started shooting other groups. But I remained a KISS fan and always bought their records as soon as they were released.

My enthusiasm picked up again when KISS came through Palm Beach in 1983 for their *Creatures of the Night* tour. It was Vinnie Vincent's debut. I met up with John Harte and asked him if I could go to the show, just to see the guys and say hello. He said, "First off, drive me to the arena."

John Harte—who was a really big guy—scrunched into my little Volkswagen Dasher and we drove over the bridge to West Palm Beach. We went into the arena and John hands me about fifty passes. The opening act that night was the Plasmatics. Backstage, the late Wendy O' Williams passed by me, but I couldn't introduce myself because I was busy putting dates on my passes.

During soundcheck I saw a lone figure sitting off to the side. Lo and behold, it's Gene Simmons! He introduced me to Vinnie (whose makeup character was an Egyptian Wizard) and I said, "I used to take photos for KISS in the olden days," and he said, "Well, these are the new-dum days."

As usual, the show was fantastic. I enjoyed seeing KISS again. Vinnie's a great guitar player but, to me, Ace is the best of all. That concert was the last time I saw KISS until the "Reunion" shows.

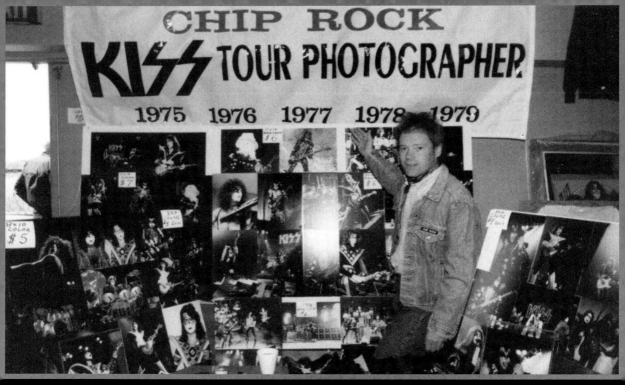

Displaying my work at one of Richie Ranno's NY KISS Conventions. Photo by Peter Dayton.

WHEN I WASN'T PHOTOGRAPHING KISS, I was still involved with the band on some level. I went to many KISS conventions and sold photos through mail order. I did it mostly for fun. Financially I just broke even.

Then in 1995, another excellent opportunity came along. I learned that KISS was self-publishing their own book named *KISStory*. I had obtained Gene's fax number from a guy at a KISS convention and I faxed him a letter saying I had many photos in my archive. A couple of nights later my phone rang. I picked up the receiver and heard, "Uncle Chip? This is Gene!" He had gotten my fax and was interested in my participating in *KISStory*.

Gene was clear about the financial arrangements—KISS wasn't offering magazine prices for photos. However, he seemed very enthusiastic about including my work in the book. He gave me an address to send my photos, which I did the next day. A few weeks later, I got a call from Gene confirming that KISS was using many of my shots and I should sign a release for publication.

Later, a member of KISS' staff called me to get my thoughts on photographing KISS during their early years. Looking back, I was very happy to know that all forty-one shots I submitted to Gene were published in *KISStory*. By the way, though some of the photos in this book may resemble shots that appear in *KISStory*, they are truly outtakes. Most haven't seen the light of day before now.

Meanwhile, I was still buying KISS records. I like Eric Singer a lot on drums, and Bruce Kulick is a great guitar player. When *KISS MTV Unplugged* came out, I thought it was a spectacular album. Every musician ever involved with KISS is great.

KISS ALIVE/ WORLDWIDE 1996-1997

I FOUND OUT ABOUT KISS' "Alive/Worldwide" reunion tour like everyone else; I happened to be watching the Grammy Awards in February 1996, and they just walked on stage in full makeup. My phone immediately rang with friends yelling, "KISS is back with makeup!" I couldn't believe it.

Through the grapevine, I found out they were indeed touring and that it was all going to start in Detroit. I faxed Gene to let him know I wanted in. When the tour was officially announced, I asked him if I could shoot a couple of their reunion shows. Their current management office called me about shooting some concerts and asked if I'd fly to Detroit. I would have loved that but we couldn't come to a financial agreement.

KISS and I picked a couple of shows in New York for me to shoot, although I didn't really want to photograph them on home ground. Ninety percent of my KISS photos were taken someplace other than the Tri-State area, and I like it that way. We decided that I would shoot the second night in Pittsburgh, Pennsylvania.

It was like time travel. Just like the old days, I was back in the car, driving three or four hundred miles to see KISS; it made me feel young again. At the Civic Arena, they had these huge, inflated KISS balloons displayed for the fans' delight. I was impressed!

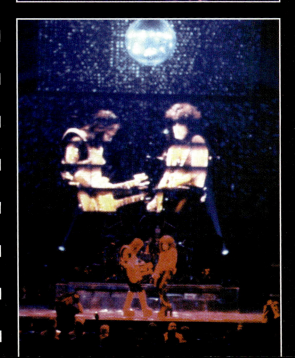

Soon a van drives up towards the gate where I was told to wait. The original KISS—Gene, Ace, Paul and Peter—pile out of this vehicle with little security (I learn that the band no longer uses limousines because they are too identifiable today). Gene walks right by me until I get his attention. He shakes my hand and waves me into a little backstage room to talk about camera angles.

Before showtime I buy the new tour program. It doesn't have any of my photos published in it, but I wanted to get an autograph for my eight-year-old son, Robby, who's impressed with KISS and my photos of them. He listens to my old KISS records, especially the first album with "Firehouse." It's like he picked up where I left off.

After the show I hang around backstage while KISS is in their dressing room with Metallica. Finally, Gene walks out, and I ask him if he would sign the tour program for Robby. He gladly obliges and asks why don't I bring my wife and sons to the New York shows. "You mean I can get passes for them?" He says, "Sure, my kids are going to be there." I was floored.

I also got Paul's autograph and complimented him on the tour. It's been almost fifteen years since I talked to KISS and saw them back in action. The new production was beyond my expectations. The precision and the professionalism were incredible. It was especially amazing to have Ace back and playing better than ever.

One of the best KISS shows was the third of four nights at Madison Square Garden. I wasn't planning to go but as the date neared I couldn't resist. At the last minute, I hopped a bus near my Long Island home to New York City to catch KISS again.

Once in the city, I happened to walk into an Irish pub. While not the most elegant bar in the world, KISS songs were played one after the other on the jukebox. "Strutter" blasted loudly, and fifty guys with Budweisers stomped and sang along. The atmosphere was incredible.

Down the block, another bar was also playing KISS music. New York was electric that night.

Considering my last-minute plans, I didn't have a ticket and I was leery of scalpers. Suddenly, someone came up to me and offered me a legitimate ticket at five dollars over face value. He had a map and could seat me where I wanted, which was about halfway up near the center in the back of the arena.

What a show that was! Paul yelled between songs, "Is this what you came for?" and the audience started roaring. I was standing at that point but had to sit down because I realized the energy these guys had on stage was more than I could handle. I respect KISS' ability to do a two-hour performance like that; I was wiped out halfway through.

After shooting KISS concerts, I always felt a mix of being worn out, exhilarated and high from the music. In the old days I'd be soaked through with sweat and have confetti stuck in my hair and stuffed down my shirt. Even after I'd shower, there was always confetti still stuck to me.

A week later I was scheduled to shoot a wedding in upstate New York on a Saturday. Coincidentally, KISS was playing Montreal, Ottawa and Toronto on the following Sunday, Monday and Tuesday. I told my wife I wouldn't be coming home after the wedding shoot; I'm going to see KISS again!

The vibes were fantastic in Ottawa; everyone was into it. The show was not as perfect as the Garden concert, but it was still good. Now I'd seen the KISS reunion from two different perspectives: up close and personal with the band, and then as a fan when I sat back and listened. It primed me for my next pass, because I knew the band's moves and could anticipate what I wanted to shoot.

I decided to start taking shots in the back, because at the Pittsburgh show I had a great opportunity for amazing shots with the video screens in the background. I learned through trial and error to reduce my shutter speed to capture images from the monitors; the video screens would break up when photographed at a faster speed.

In October I got the band's approval to shoot the Albany show at the Knickerbocker Arena. The band was looking a little ragged earlier in the day, but the show was fantastic.

I was everywhere that night, just like the old days—the photo pit, the audience and on the soundboard. I shot "Deuce" way up in the back of the arena with a tripod.

Sometimes when I was up in the rafters setting up a shot, I'd have to show my "Working Band" pass. Fans in the vicinity would gather around me asking questions. I showed them the set list and they couldn't believe they were getting a sneak preview of that night's show. They begged me for the copy, but I didn't turn it over to them.

My biggest thrill ever in my years of photographing KISS occurred at that show. Tommy Thayer, the band coordinator, came to me with an idea: He said that after Peter finished his solo spotlights illuminated the crowd, so I would have a good photo opportunity to shoot Peter from behind the drum set. I was surprised and honored that Tommy asked me to shoot this particular photograph. I put myself in the back of the arena for the opening numbers—shots of Ace's smoking guitar solo, Gene flying and so on. After seeing a couple of shows, I was pretty keyed into the timing.

Then comes the greatest shot of all. Tommy is waiting for me behind the stage area. As Peter is doing his solo, we position ourselves behind him. Peter finishes his solo, stands up and flashes his sticks in the air. The stage lights come up and flood the arena. From behind me, I hear "NOW!"

I was sure I had gotten the shot. When I got the film developed—wow! It was unbelievable. I look back on all those years of driving, shooting, standing in the rain and developing the shots. I remember the music, the darkened arenas, the screaming fans—the excitement and electricity of KISS, all summarized in that photo of Peter!

I look forward to new KISS projects because they may give me a chance to photograph them again. There's nothing else in the world I'd rather do than photograph a KISS concert.

EPILOGUE

By August 1999, I had finished my work on *Outtakes* and was in the midst of some "fine-tuning" with the publisher. I was basically satisfied that the last chapter you just read was a fitting ending to this book. I wasn't thinking of adding an Epilogue until the night of August 12.

In mid-August advertisements were running on television and in newspapers heralding the opening of *Detroit Rock City*, KISS' first full-length feature film. The day before *Detroit Rock City* was released, I found myself on Block Island, a small summer resort fifteen miles from Montauk, New York. As I walked down a crowded Water Street near the ferry dock, I noticed an image of KISS on a poster in a storefront window. "Must be for the movie," I thought to myself. As I got closer, I could read "Tonight at Captain Nick's—Canada's number-one KISS tribute band, 'Dressed to Kill.'" I was going!

In all my twenty-five years of following KISS, I had never seen a KISS tribute band. But this time I wanted to see "Dressed to Kill." Then I thought, "Hey, I'll bring my camera along, too." I was "on island"—as they say there—for a professional photo shoot so I had my good equipment with me.

The night club and bar scene on Block Island during the high summer season is considered to be the best in New England. (Block Island is part of the state of Rhode Island.) If not the best, then certainly the wildest. Over ten different bars, all within walking distance in the downtown area, are packed with vacationers and locals alike every night.

I arrived at Captain Nick's early to try and meet someone with the band. I ended up being invited by the house management to shoot a "staff photo," the entire staff with "Dressed to Kill." Soon I realized everyone was calling them "KISS" as in "I can't wait for the KISS concert to start." I really got a kick out of that.

As I waited for the call to go backstage, I admired the equipment set up. I noticed the Marshall "cabs" on the right and the flashpots set up in front of the drums. I thought to myself, "Well, if they can't play (as in play well), at least I'll see some fire and hear some bombs go off. Moments later a roadie lead me to a back room filled with the staff waiting for the band to come in the back door. All of a sudden "Gene" and "Paul" walked in. The vibes were almost as special as being in the dressing room at Cobo Hall in 1975. And as I clicked off a couple of shots of everyone, I started to feel as if it might really be "one of those hot nights!" As the band walked down a steep flight of stairs toward the stage, on the spur of the moment I just followed along. Just like I used to do with KISS in the "old days." What a blast! I then headed for the balcony to check out the first tune. I was hoping for "Deuce" and sure enough the first chords rang out of one of the greatest rock and roll songs of all time. And it did sound good—note for note— perfect to the original with all the feeling and energy of the real KISS. While listening to "Got to Choose," all the feelings I got on that beach in Puerto Rico twenty-four years ago came back to me. "Peter's" drumming was excellent. His upper body hardly moving, with a smirk on his face, but his arms flailing about all over his kit. "Paul" had all the moves down too, even his voice rang true. And Gene—the strut, the tongue, and the original Gibson "Ripper" bass that Gene played when I first saw him at the Beacon—was perfect. He really played the part right up to the end of "Firehouse," when he breathed fire. As he stuck the sword into the log on the floor, the no-so-sweet smell of kerosene permeated the stage area. Other songs I especially liked were "100,000 Years," and "Shock Me" with "Ace" playing a very hot solo.

So it turned into a fun night for all. "Dressed to Kill" had flooded me with great memories as I realized they and other KISS tribute bands exist to keep the spirit and energy of KISS alive forever.